**Be a
Community
Leader**

# How to
# Stay Informed

Leslie Harper

**PowerKiDS**
press.
New York

Published in 2015 by The Rosen Publishing Group, Inc.
29 East 21st Street, New York, NY 10010

First Edition

Editor: Norman D. Graubart
Book Design: Joe Carney
Book Layout: Colleen Bialecki
Photo Research: Katie Stryker

Photo Credits: Cover Brian Davis/PhotoLlibrary/Getty Images; p. 4 Win McNamee/Getty Images; p. 5 BrianAJackson/iStock/Thinkstock; p. 6 Jetta Productions/Photodisc/Thinkstock; p. 7 Dmitriy Shironosov/iStock/Thinkstock; p. 8 MikeCherim/iStock/Thinkstock; p. 9 Fuse/Thinkstock; p. 10 raywoo/iStock/Thinkstock; p. 11 shootsphoto/iStock/Thinkstock; p. 13 themorningglor/iStock/Thinkstock; p. 14 Vladone/iStock/Thinkstock; pp. 15, 21 Monkey Business Images/Thinkstock; p. 16 Zeynep Ozyurek/iStock/Thinkstock; p. 17 Tetra Images/Thinkstock; p. 18 Steve Debenport/E+/Getty Images; p. 19 Sam Bloomberg-Rissman/Blend Images/Getty Images; p. 20 Oleksit Maksymenko/All Canada Photos/Getty Images; p. 22 pablocalvog/iStock/Thinkstock; p. 23 Nadine Rupp/Getty Images; p. 25 martiapunts/iStock/Thinkstock; p. 26 PhotoAlto/Frederic Cirou/Vetta/Getty Images; p. 28 db2stock/Getty Images; p. 29 Photodisc/Thinkstock; p. 30 Ariel Skelley/Blend Images/Getty Images.

Library of Congress Cataloging-in-Publication Data

Harper, Leslie.
 How to stay informed / by Leslie Harper. — 1st ed.
    pages cm. — (Be a community leader)
 Includes index.
 ISBN 978-1-4777-6701-6 (library binding) — ISBN 978-1-4777-6702-3 (pbk.) —
ISBN 978-1-4777-6703-0 (6-pack)
 1. Mass media—Research—United States—Juvenile literature. 2. Library orientation for children—United States—Juvenile literature. 3. Electronic information resource searching—United States—Juvenile literature. 4. Citizenship—United States—Juvenile literature. I. Title.
 P91.5.U5H37 2015
 302.23—dc23
                                           2014006320

Manufactured in the United States of America

CPSIA Compliance Information: Batch #WS14PK3: For Further Information contact Rosen Publishing, New York, New York at 1-800-237-9932

# Contents

# Get in the Know

The system of government in which people choose leaders that make and enforce laws is called a **democracy**. To choose the best leaders, people in a democracy need to know what is going on in the world, in their country, and in their community. There are many ways to stay informed, such as reading newspapers, news magazines, and **credible**, or trustworthy, websites. When you reach the age of 18, you will use these sources to decide how you will vote in elections.

Here, President Barack Obama meets French president François Hollande. News organizations report on these types of meetings every day.

NEWS

BUSINESS NEWS
GLOBAL MARKETS
EMPLOYMENT
TECHNOLOGY

**Many print newspapers are also available online or as tablet and smartphone apps.**

However, staying informed is about more than voting. Staying informed is a basic part of being a citizen. Knowledge about the world is a tool you can use to change your community. It can also help you change the minds of people in power. To achieve these goals, you will need to learn how to **interpret**, or understand the true meaning of, information. You will also need to find good sources. Then, you can use technology and your own voice to get the word out. This book will help you learn these skills!

# Understanding Media

Most people use some form of **media** to stay informed about current events and the world around them. Media is the means through which facts are told to others. Most of the information presented in the media is gathered and written by **journalists**. Journalists have a very important job. They investigate news stories and gather facts. They speak to people involved in the stories and learn about the different views those people might hold. Journalists then organize all the information they have gathered and present it in ways that readers can understand.

This library has computers with which one can access websites. Library computers also have programs that let you look for books in the library.

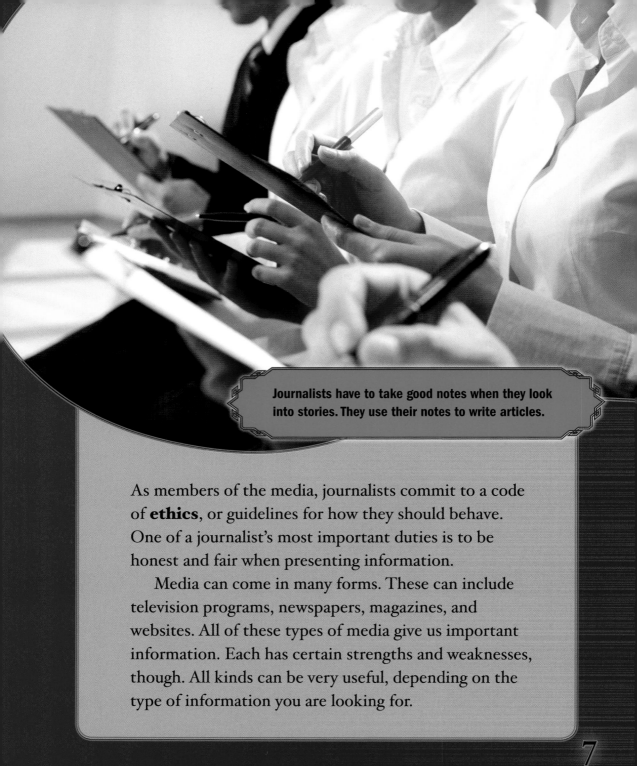

Journalists have to take good notes when they look into stories. They use their notes to write articles.

As members of the media, journalists commit to a code of **ethics**, or guidelines for how they should behave. One of a journalist's most important duties is to be honest and fair when presenting information.

Media can come in many forms. These can include television programs, newspapers, magazines, and websites. All of these types of media give us important information. Each has certain strengths and weaknesses, though. All kinds can be very useful, depending on the type of information you are looking for.

One of the best ways to stay informed about current events is by reading newspapers. National newspapers cover topics that would be of interest to people all around the country. Local newspapers include some national and world news. However, they focus mostly on events and information that would be of interest to people living in a certain area. Most towns and cities have at least one local paper, and many have several.

In recent years, the Internet has become a major source of news. Unlike print sources, websites can be edited and updated many times a day, as soon as new information becomes available. One kind of website, called a **blog**, often shares links to news stories as well as people's experiences and opinions.

Television journalists can report from where an event is happening. This can make reports about things such as severe weather more interesting.

Some radio stations also have news broadcasts. Other stations report the news all day long.

Blogs tend to focus on one topic. Blogs cover single issues like climate change or immigration. People who want to tell the world about something they are involved in, such as an organic farm, often keep blogs. These blogs may cover issues on the farm, and also link to news stories about the larger world of organic farming.

## Tips for Staying Informed

*For most of history, people learned information by word of mouth. Later, important texts were copied by hand, but this took a lot of time. Then, in the fifteenth century, Johannes Gutenberg invented the printing press, which used movable type. This machine allowed thousands of copies of a page of text to be printed in a single day. The printing press made it possible for newspapers to be published every day.*

# Understanding Texts

To stay informed, people must be able to understand the news they read and watch. Understanding an article is easier when you can break it down and identify the pieces. A news article should include information such as who is the subject of the story, what happened, when it happened, where it happened, and why it happened. This information, which answers the questions who, what, when, where, and why, is called the five w's. Articles should also include supporting facts. An article might say, for example, that some town residents were upset by a plan to knock down

If you read a news article that doesn't answer these questions, then it probably doesn't come from a credible source.

Who
What
Why
Wher
Wher

a historic building. To support, or prove, that statement, the article might say that 30 people spoke out against the plan at a town meeting.

Usually, news reporters do not include their own opinions or thoughts. Sometimes, though, you may read an article that does include opinions. If the article uses phrases such as "I think" or "I feel," then it includes opinions. This does not make the information in the article wrong. However, the author may be telling only part of the story.

Be aware that some pieces might look like news articles, but actually are not. Sometimes, writers like to make their opinion pieces appear to be news stories.

## Tips for Staying Informed

Facts are things that are always true, while opinions are things that only some people believe. News articles often report on peoples' opinions. They do this by using quotations. A quotation, or quote, is something that a person says that is then repeated exactly. A quote from a town resident explaining his opinion that knocking down a historic building is a terrible idea would support the fact that some in town are upset about the plan.

# Finding Good Sources

Staying informed means starting with good information. Credible information comes from credible sources. Not all sources provide credible information. This is true of newspapers, television programs, and magazines. However, it is especially true of the Internet. This is because anyone can create a website and include any information he chooses. Unfortunately, many websites provide information that is untrue or outdated. Websites run by local or federal governments, universities, and news organizations with good reputations are great places to get credible information.

To decide if a source is credible, start by looking at the author's background. Is the author of the piece trained as a journalist? If not, does she have an education in another field that would make her an expert on the topic, such as finance or science? You should also try to determine if the author has a **bias**, or preference for a certain opinion. For example, a doctor may write an article about how well a certain medicine works. However, if the doctor works for the company that sells that medicine, he may not be a credible source.

**500571 – 501900**

The reference section of a library has books you can use to look up people, places, and ideas that you read about in news articles.

The style of an article is also a good clue as to whether it is coming from a credible source. Articles published in magazines and newspapers have been read over by **editors**. Editors look for any mistakes in spelling and grammar, as well as correct any parts of the article that do not make sense. Most published articles are also read by fact-checkers. These people look up each fact stated in the article to make sure that it is true. As you read through an article, keep an eye out for spelling and grammar mistakes. If you spot several, it does not mean the information is untrue. It is a clue, however, that the article has not been edited and fact-checked by people other than the author.

Some buildings in Washington, DC, house government offices. Government organizations are reliable sources of information.

You should also note if the article uses supporting facts from credible sources. If the author includes facts and numbers, such as the number of people in the United States who carpool to work, those numbers should come from a credible source, such as the US Department of Transportation.

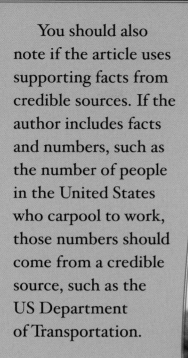

College professors do more than teach classes. Most professors also do research and publish articles and books. These are usually reliable sources.

## Tips for Staying Informed

In most cases, anyone who is quoted in an article should be named. Knowing whom the quotation comes from lets people decide if it is information they can trust. If the person is not named, readers cannot make that decision. In some cases, however, the source of a quotation is kept secret because that person is afraid of getting in trouble.

# Avoiding Bad Sources

When you know what makes a good source, it is easier to spot bad sources. Bad sources present information that is outdated, biased, or simply incorrect. If you think you may be using a bad source, you can become your own fact-checker! If the article **cites**, or states, where it got the information it is using, track those facts down. Go to the source's website and try to find the facts yourself. By looking at the website, you can also better determine if that source itself is credible. If the author of the article you are reading does not say where she got her information, and there is not a way to check it, then you should find another source.

Even if the source you are reading isn't online, you can use the Internet to check facts. Academic websites and other news sites can help you do this.

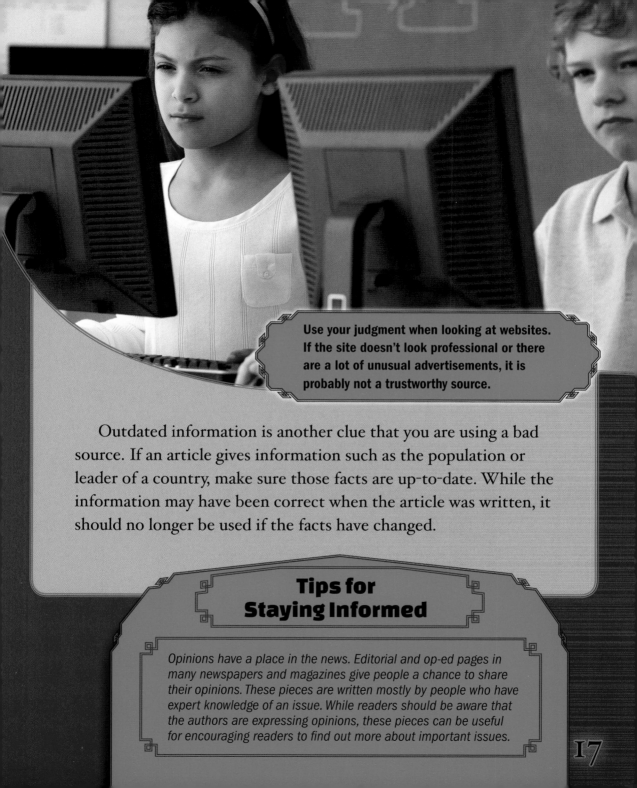

Use your judgment when looking at websites. If the site doesn't look professional or there are a lot of unusual advertisements, it is probably not a trustworthy source.

Outdated information is another clue that you are using a bad source. If an article gives information such as the population or leader of a country, make sure those facts are up-to-date. While the information may have been correct when the article was written, it should no longer be used if the facts have changed.

## Tips for Staying Informed

Opinions have a place in the news. Editorial and op-ed pages in many newspapers and magazines give people a chance to share their opinions. These pieces are written mostly by people who have expert knowledge of an issue. While readers should be aware that the authors are expressing opinions, these pieces can be useful for encouraging readers to find out more about important issues.

# Libraries and Librarians

Knowing what types of sources to use to stay informed is important. It is also important to know where to find these sources. Your school library and local library are great places to start. They contain books on nearly every topic you can think of. They also generally have current editions of many newspapers and magazines. Many libraries also keep past editions of some newspapers, either in print or as digital copies.

Reference librarians help people find information. They are trained to help people like you use library materials.

This is the periodical section of a library. Periodicals are magazines, newspapers, and other media that are published on a regular schedule.

If you are unsure where to start, talk to your local librarian or school media specialist. Librarians are trained and have a lot of experience in finding and organizing information. They can help you find copies of newspapers and help you search online databases for more information. Online databases keep track of information about all kinds of issues. There are online databases for everything from movies to wars.

The large amount of information contained in a library is just the beginning. A librarian can help you narrow your search for important information and steer you in the right direction.

# Using Computers

It may take months for a book about a current event to be published and make its way to your local library. Most newspapers are published once a day, and magazines may be published once a week, once a month, or on another schedule. The Internet, on the other hand, can bring you up-to-date information in just seconds. Because of this, a computer or tablet can be a useful tool to keep you informed. Like finding information in a library, searching the Internet for information is all about knowing where to look.

Google is the most popular search engine. Google will give you a lot of results for your searches, so be sure to pick good sources when you do research.

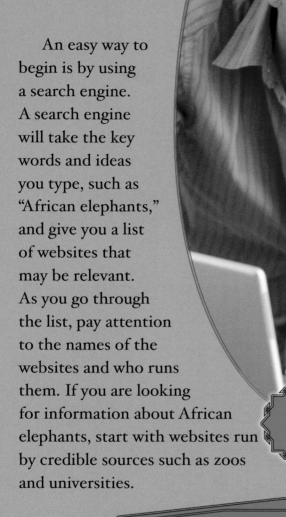

An easy way to begin is by using a search engine. A search engine will take the key words and ideas you type, such as "African elephants," and give you a list of websites that may be relevant. As you go through the list, pay attention to the names of the websites and who runs them. If you are looking for information about African elephants, start with websites run by credible sources such as zoos and universities.

You can ask your parents to help you use the Internet safely.

## Tips for Staying Informed

*Search engines can give you tens or hundreds of results. It is still up to you to pick credible sources. The ending of a website's name can quickly tell you more about the group that runs it. Government websites end with ".gov." College and university websites end with ".edu," and nonprofit groups' sites end with ".org."*

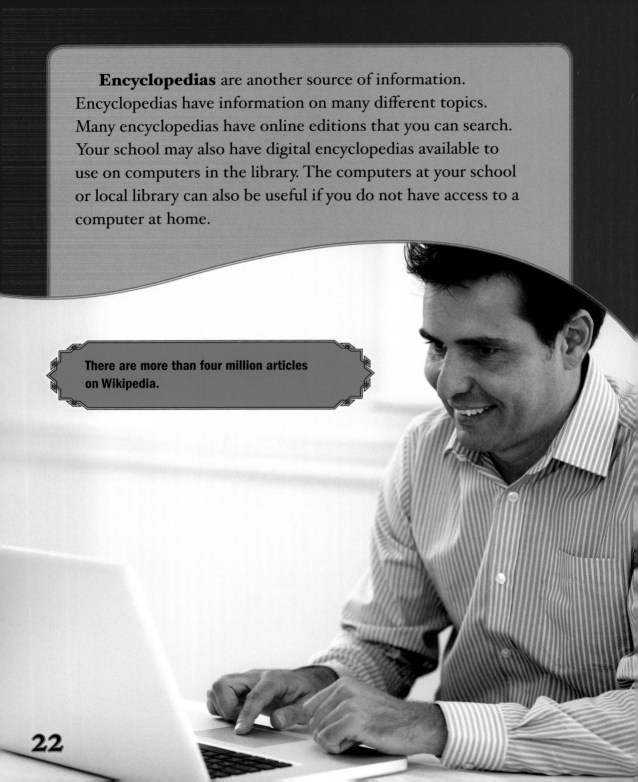

**Encyclopedias** are another source of information. Encyclopedias have information on many different topics. Many encyclopedias have online editions that you can search. Your school may also have digital encyclopedias available to use on computers in the library. The computers at your school or local library can also be useful if you do not have access to a computer at home.

There are more than four million articles on Wikipedia.

One popular online encyclopedia is Wikipedia. Wikipedia is easy to use. However, Wikipedia can be edited by anybody. This means that someone who is not an expert or who is biased about a subject can edit a Wikipedia article. People who feel strongly about a subject can edit its page to make their opinions look like facts. Wikipedia pages about presidents or political issues, for example, are often biased. You can use Wikipedia to begin your search for information, but always look at the sources listed at the bottom of the page. By going to those websites, you can see where the online editors got their information.

# So Much Information!

Sometimes it may seem there is just too much information out there to stay completely informed. It is true that today we have access to more information than ever before in history. However, each newspaper, magazine, and website only has so much room to report the news. The space on the page is limited, so each newspaper or website cannot report on everything that happens. As a result, most journalists focus only on a certain area of news. Therefore, to stay well informed, you will have to use multiple sources. When looking through possible sources, choose a few that are credible and that you enjoy reading. If you are using the Internet, you can use apps to create a Rich Site Summary, or RSS, feed. An RSS feed will show you **headlines** and short descriptions of articles from many different websites.

One benefit of reading multiple sources is that you can check the information you read in one source against the information in another. In fact, it is always a good idea to find at least two sources that agree on each fact you find. This will help you determine if facts are true and up-to-date.

There are many smartphone apps that will manage an RSS feed.

# See It for Yourself

Using media sources, such as newspapers, magazines, and websites, is a great way to stay informed. However, it is not the only way. You can also witness news events in person.

If you are interested in local news that affects your community, there are many ways to stay informed. Start by learning more about how your local government works. Many cities are run by city councils. These are groups of elected officials who make laws and decisions about an area. If your city is led by a city council, see if you can attend one of their meetings.

If you want to stay informed about issues that affect your school, try attending a meeting of the local school board. Another thing you can do is run for student council. The student council, like a city council, helps make decisions that affect a school. By being on the student council, you will get a chance to learn more about and discuss issues. If there are any issues you feel strongly about, talk them over with your teachers and principal.

These students are reading their school newspaper. Writing for your school newspaper can help keep your whole school informed about important issues.

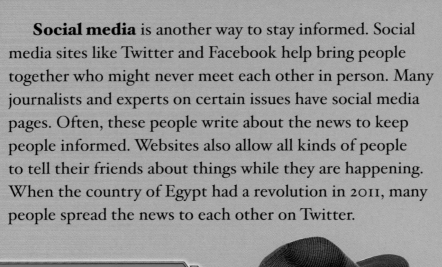

Social media is another way to stay informed. Social media sites like Twitter and Facebook help bring people together who might never meet each other in person. Many journalists and experts on certain issues have social media pages. Often, these people write about the news to keep people informed. Websites also allow all kinds of people to tell their friends about things while they are happening. When the country of Egypt had a revolution in 2011, many people spread the news to each other on Twitter.

These kids are talking to a park ranger about local environmental issues. Talking to experts is always a good way to stay informed.

In addition to using social media to learn about what's going on in your community, you can use it to spread the word yourself! Twitter lets you use up to 140 characters, or letters and spaces, in each tweet, or post. This is a good way to practice journalism. For example, if you want to report on a story, you can make each tweet one of the five w's. In one tweet, you can describe the "who" of your story, then the next tweets will be the "what," "where," "when," and "why" of your story.

If you talk to someone in person about an important issue, try to take notes. It's easier to remember your conversation if you have important facts written down!

29

# Knowledge Is Power

The United States functions best when its citizens and residents stay informed and get involved. That means people have a responsibility to be informed and make good decisions for their neighborhood, state, and country. The more informed you are about important issues, the more **empowered** you are as a citizen.

Staying informed can help you be an active member of your school and community. It will also help you when you are old enough to vote. Reading newspaper and magazine articles, looking through news websites, and attending meetings of your local government can introduce you to important issues. Most importantly, you can share your opinions and supporting facts and keep everyone else informed. School newspapers and social media offer every student the chance to report the news.

Staying informed will help you do well in school. You never know when issues from current events will find their way into your history or science class!

# Glossary

**bias** (BY-us) An unfair preference for or dislike of something or someone.

**blog** (BLOG) A personal website on which someone writes about his or her thoughts and opinions and shares links.

**cites** (SYTS) Calls attention to or gives credit to a source.

**credible** (KREH-duh-bel) Believable and trustworthy.

**democracy** (dih-MAH-kruh-see) A system of government whereby people choose leaders and participate in making laws through an election process.

**editors** (EH-dih-terz) The people who correct mistakes, check facts, and decide what will be printed in a newspaper, book, or magazine.

**empowered** (im-POW-erd) Having power.

**encyclopedias** (in-sy-kluh-PEE-dee-uhz) Books that have information about a wide range of subjects, usually in alphabetical order.

**ethics** (EH-thiks) The study of what is good and bad and how people should behave.

**headlines** (HED-lynz) The titles, written in large letters, of stories in newspapers or magazines.

**interpret** (in-TER-prit) To explain the meaning.

**journalists** (JER-nul-ists) People who gather and write news for a newspaper or magazine.

**media** (MEE-dee-uh) The means, such as TV and newspapers, through which facts are told to others.

**social media** (SOH-shul MEE-dee-uh) Online communities through which people share information, messages, photos, videos, and thoughts.

# Index

# Websites

Due to the changing nature of Internet links, PowerKids Press has developed an online list of websites related to the subject of this book. This site is updated regularly. Please use this link to access the list: www.powerkidslinks.com/beacl/inform/